Dominick Argento
Three Sonnets of Petrarch

for Baritone and Piano

BOOSEY & HAWKES

DISTRIBUTED BY

HAL•LEONARD®
CORPORATION
7777 W. BLUEMOUND RD. P.O. BOX 13819 MILWAUKEE, WI 53213

www.boosey.com
www.halleonard.com

Commissioned jointly by the BBC and the Royal Philharmonic Society
as part of BBC Radio 3's New Generation Artists Scheme

First performance:
Ronan Collett, baritone
Tom Poster, piano
The Cheltenham Festival
Pittville Pump Room, Cheltenham, UK
July 14, 2007

CONTENTS

Composer's Note

I chose these three sonnets to represent the beginning, middle and end of Petrarch's unrequited love for a married woman named Laura. Whether the Laura who inspired the poet's celebrated verses was an actual person or a poetic device long associated with the idealization of women is a question that has divided scholars for centuries and is not likely ever to be settled to the satisfaction of all. Consequently, before I felt prepared to put music to these sonnets I had to address that question and take a stand. On the basis of Petrarch's original language—unstilted and passionate— and a denial he makes in a letter to a friend who accused him of 'inventing' Laura ("I wish that she indeed had been a fiction and not a madness...") I opted to consider her a real person. Therefore, I assumed that Petrarch's passion for Laura was sincere, profound and abiding. The music I have written for these sonnets is a product of that view.

Dominick Argento

Vocal Texts

I. Sonnet 63 (Volgendo gli occhi)

Volgendo gli occhi al mio novo colore,
che fa di morte rimembrar la gente,
pietà vi mosse; onde, benignamente
salutando, teneste in vita il core.

La fraile vita ch'ancor meco alberga,
fu de' begli occhi vostri aperto dono,
e de la voce angelica soave.
Da lor conosco l'esser ov'io sono:

ché, come suol pigro animal per verga,
cosí destaro in me l'anima grave.
Del mio cor, donna, l'una e l'altra chiave

avete in mano; e di ciò son contento,
presto di navigare a ciascun vento;
ch'ogni cosa da voi m'è dolce onore.

Casting eyes upon my newfound paleness,
people cannot help but think of death,
yet you were moved by pity; whereupon
my heart, greeted so gently, clung to life.

The fragile life that lodges within me still
was a gift freely bestowed by a glance from your beautiful eyes,
and by the sweet and gentle voice of an angel.
To them, I know, my being owes existence:

As exhausted sheep respond to the shepherd's prod,
thus, my weighed down soul was also aroused.
My heart, dear lady, is unlocked only with those keys

in your possession; of that I am content,
and ready to live in whatever condition you please;
to me, your every gift is honor sweet.

II. Sonnet 164 (Or che 'l ciel)

Or che 'l ciel e la terra e 'l vento tace
e le fere e gli augelli il sonno affrena,
Notte il carro stellato in giro mena,
e nel suo letto il mar senz'onda giace,

vegghio, penso, ardo, piango; e chi mi sface
sempre m'è inanzi per mia dolce pena:
guerra è 'l mio stato, d'ira e di duol piena,
e sol di lei pensando ho qualche pace.

Così sol d'una chiara fonte viva
move 'l dolce e l'amaro ond'io mi pasco;
una man sola mi risana e punge;

e perché 'l mio martir non giunga a riva,
mille volte il dí moro e mille nasco,
tanto da la salute mia son lunge.

Now that sky and earth and wind are hushed
and beasts and birds in sleep are silenced too,
Night steers its starry chariot through its course
and even the waveless sea retires to bed.

I see, I think, I burn, I weep, and she, my undoer,
is ever before my eyes as sweet punishment:
I wage a war against myself in anger and pain,
and only in thoughts of her do I find peace.

And thus it is that from one clear living fountain come
both the bitter and the sweet whereon I am sustained;
A single hand both stabs me and also heals the wound;

and that is why my suffering will never cease,
I die yet am reborn a thousand times a day,
while release from pain remains far, far away.

III. Sonnet 300 (Quanta invidia io ti porto)

Quanta invidia io ti porto, avara terra,
ch'abbracci quella cui veder m'è tolto,
e mi contendi l'aria del bel volto,
dove pace trovai d'ogni mia guerra!

Quanta ne porto al ciel, che chiude e serra
e sí cupidamente ha in sé raccolto
lo spirto da le belle membra sciolto,
e per altrui sí rado si diserra!

Quanta invidia a quell'anime che 'n sorte
hanno or sua santa e dolce compagnia,
la qual io cercai sempre con tal brama!

Quant'a la dispietata e dura Morte,
ch'avendo spento in lei la vita mia,
stassi ne' suoi begli occhi, e mi non chiama!

What a grudge I hold against you, selfish earth,
embracing her of whose sight I am deprived,
denying me the look of the lovely face
where, after all my strife, I had found peace!

What a grudge I hold against a heaven that shuts and
locks its gates, and with such greediness, received
with open arms the spirit of her graceful form
while for others, the gates are seldom unlocked!

What a grudge I hold against those fortunate souls
who enjoy the pleasure of her sweet and holy company
which I, with the utmost eagerness, had always sought!

What a grudge I hold against hard and pitiless Death
who, having extinguished my life through her,
now dwells in her lovely eyes and does not send for me!

Francesco Petrarch
(translated by the composer)

for Pat Solstad

Three Sonnets of Petrarch
I. Sonnet 63 (Volgendo gli occhi)

FRANCESCO PETRARCH

DOMINICK ARGENTO

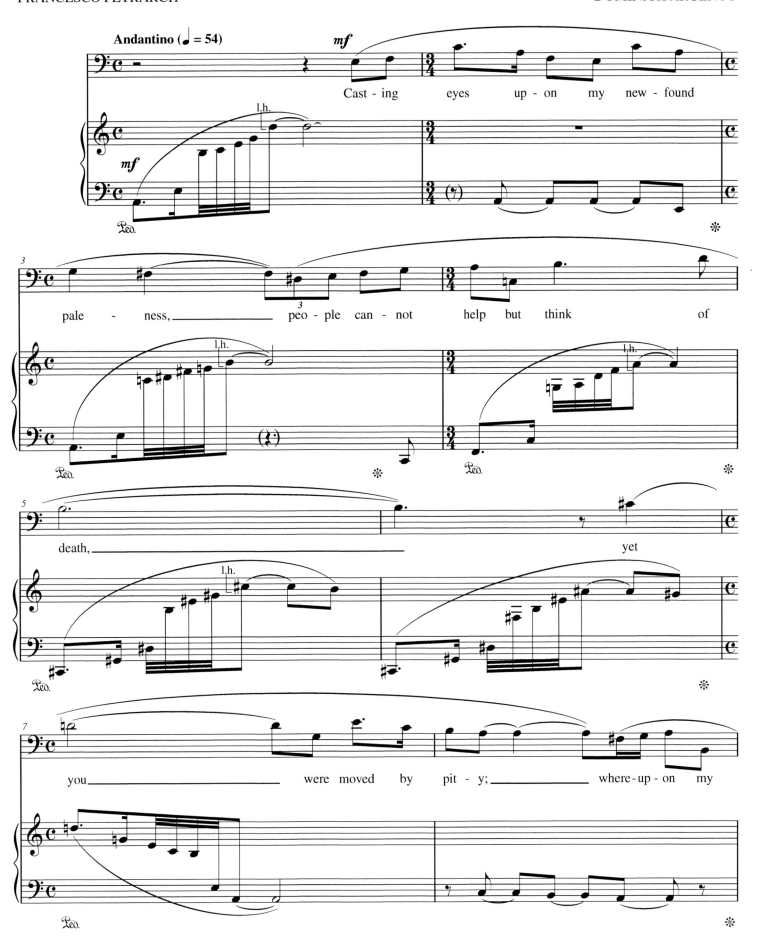

sweet and gent - le voice of an an - gel.____

To them, I know, my be - ing owes ex -

- ist - ence:_____ As ex - haust - ed sheep re - spond to the

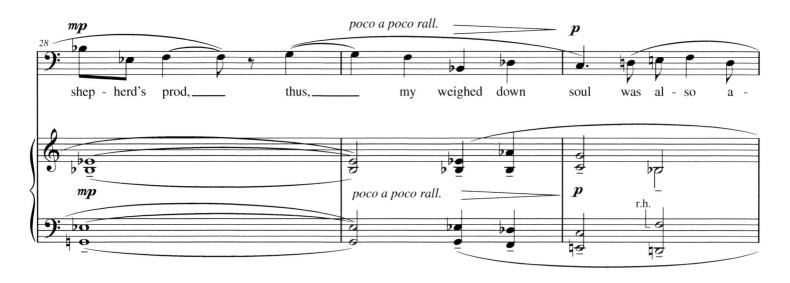

shep - herd's prod,_____ thus,_____ my weighed down soul was al - so a -

- roused._____ My heart, dear la - dy,_____ is un - locked on - ly with those

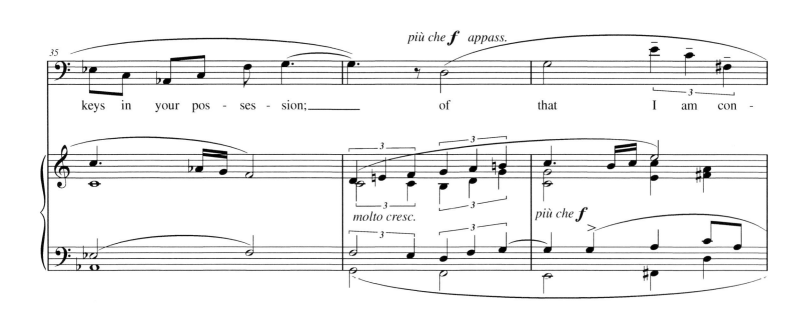

keys in your pos - ses - sion;_____ of that I am con -

- tent, _____ and read - y to live in what - ev - er con - di - tion you

please; _____ to me, your ev - 'ry gift is

hon - or sweet. _____

II. Sonnet 164 (Or che 'l ciel)

Moderato (♩ = 76)

pp tranquillo

sempre pochino a pochino cresc.

sempre pochino a pochino cresc.

Now that sky and earth and wind are hushed___ and beasts and

p

(poch. a poch. cresc.)

birds in sleep are si-lenced too,_____ Night steers its star - ry char-i-ot_____

(mp)

poco marc.

(mp)

(poch. a poch. cresc.)

___through its course_____ and e-ven the wave-less sea____ re - tires to bed.____

(poch. a poch. cresc.)

I see, ___ I think,
I burn, ___ I weep, ___ and she, ___ my un-do-er, is e-ver be-fore my
eyes as sweet pun-ish-ment: ___ I wage a war ___ a-gainst my-self in an-ger and
pain, ___ and on-ly in thoughts of her do I find peace. ___

And thus it is that from one clear liv - ing foun - tain ___ come both the bit - ter ___ and the sweet where - on I am sus - tained; ___ A sin - gle hand both stabs me ___ and al - so ___ heals the wound; ___

Poco trattenuto

3'30" ca.

III. Sonnet 300 (Quanta invidia io ti porto)

greed - i - ness, _____ re - ceived with o - pen arms the

spir - it of her grace - ful form while for

o - thers, _____ the gates are sel - dom un - locked! _____

Molto meno mosso ($\mathbf{d}$ = 40 ca.)

Poco più mosso che tempo primo ($\mathbf{d}$ = 82 ca.)

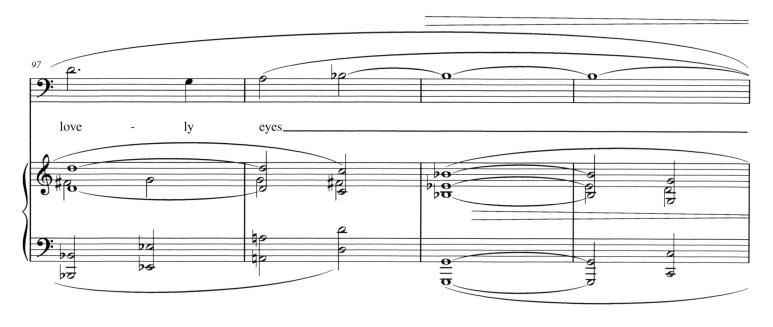

love - ly eyes

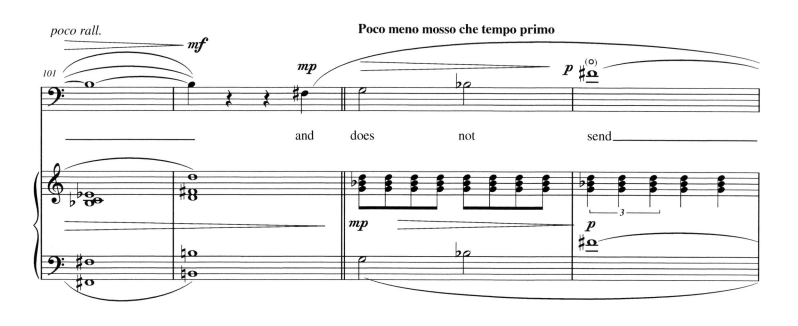

poco rall.   *mf*   **Poco meno mosso che tempo primo**   *mp*   *p*

and   does   not   send

mp   *p*

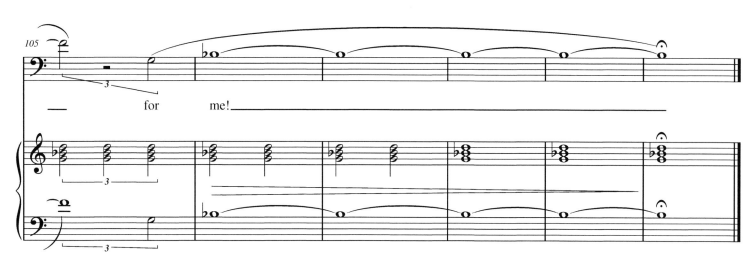

for me!

3'05''